Rookie
Read-About® Holidays

Chanukah

D1065530

By Trudi Strain Trueit

Reading Consultant
Cecilia Minden-Cupp, PhD
Former Director of the Language and Literacy Program
Harvard Graduate School of Education
Cambridge, Massachusetts

Children's Press®
A Division of Scholastic Inc.
New York   Toronto   London   Auckland   Sydney
Mexico City   New Delhi   Hong Kong
Danbury, Connecticut

Designer: Herman Adler
Photo Researcher: Caroline Anderson
The photo on the cover shows a young boy with a menorah.

Library of Congress Cataloging-in-Publication Data

Trueit, Trudi Strain.
  Chanukah / by Trudi Strain Trueit.
    p. cm. — (Rookie read-about holidays)
  ISBN 10: 0-531-12452-5 (lib. bdg.)   0-531-11833-9 (pbk.)
  ISBN 13: 978-0-531-12452-9 (lib. bdg.)   978-0-531-11833-7 (pbk.)
  1. Hanukkah—Juvenile literature. I. Title. II. Series.
  BM695.H3T74 2006
  296.4'35—dc22   2006005297

© 2007 by Scholastic Inc.
All rights reserved. Published simultaneously in Canada.
Printed in China.

CHILDREN'S PRESS, and ROOKIE READ-ABOUT®, and associated
logos are trademarks and/or registered trademarks of Scholastic Library
Publishing. SCHOLASTIC and associated logos are trademarks and/or
registered trademarks of Scholastic Inc.
6 7 8 9 10 R 16 15 14 13 12 11 10 09 08   62

People who belong to the Jewish religion celebrate Chanukah (HAH-nuh-kuh). It is a holiday when people remember a miracle.

Some people tried to force the Jews to give up their religion two thousand years ago. They formed an army that took over a Jewish temple. A temple is a place of worship where people pray and learn.

An ancient Jewish temple in Israel

The Maccabees during battle

A group of Jewish people
fought back. They were
known as the Maccabees
(MACK-uh-beez). The
Maccabees won the
battle. They returned
to their temple.

The Maccabees wanted to rededicate, or bless the temple. The word *Chanukah* means "dedication." Sadly, there was only enough oil to light the temple lamp for one day. But somehow the oil kept the lamp burning for eight days.

An oil lamp

December 2008

Sunday	Monday	Tuesday	Wednesday	Thursday	Friday	Saturday
	1	2	3	4	5	6
7	8	9	10	11	12	13
14	15	16	17	18	19	20
21	22	23	24	25	26	27
28	29	30	31			

Chanukah lasts eight days in honor of this miracle. It usually falls in December. The dates change each year.

Chanukah is also called the Festival of Lights or the Feast of Dedication.

Families light a menorah (muh-NOR-uh) each night during Chanukah. A menorah is a candleholder.

The menorah holds eight candles, plus a shamash (SHAH-mush), or "servant" candle. The shamash is used only to light the other candles.

A menorah made for children

The shamash (red candle) is used to light the other candles.

14

Special blessings are said before the menorah is lit. The shamash and one other candle are lit on the first night of Chanukah. This continues every night until all the candles are lit.

Ways to Celebrate

Chanukah is celebrated
in every country on Earth
where Jewish people live.
This includes the United
States, Israel, France,
Canada, and Russia. People
attend concerts, parades,
and menorah-lighting
ceremonies during this
festive holiday.

A Chanukah celebration in Washington, D.C.

A giant menorah in Israel

A large menorah is lit in front of the Eiffel Tower in France.

Israel holds a torch race. The torch is passed from one runner to the next as it goes from town to town. At the end of the race, the torch is used to light a menorah in Jerusalem.

Menorahs are made
from all kinds of things,
including balloons,
chocolate, and seashells.
One was carved from ice
in Russia.

Some Jewish families
create their own
menorahs for Chanukah.
The candleholders can
be made from clay, wood,
or even a potato!

A handmade menorah

Friends celebrating Chanukah together

Some families sing a song after the menorah is lit. They may tell the story of the first Chanukah. Other families like to share what it means to be Jewish.

Special foods are eaten during Chanukah. Potato pancakes called latkes (LAHT-kuhz) are popular in America.

A favorite treat in Israel is sufganiyot (soof-gahn-YOTE). These are similar to jelly donuts covered with powdered sugar.

Sufganiyot

A dreidel

Many children are
given small gifts during
Chanukah. They may get
books, chocolate coins,
or a dreidel (DRAY-del).
A dreidel is a square
top with a Hebrew letter
on each side. Hebrew is
the language of the
Jewish people.

Dreidel is a fun game.
The letter the player lands
on tells the person what
to do next.

Some people throw
Chanukah parties. Families
often serve latkes, butter
cookies, and pretzels. They
sing, dance, and play dreidel.
It is a very joyful time.

A child playing dreidel

Words You Know

celebrate

dreidel

Hebrew

Maccabees

menorah

oil lamp

shamash

temple

Index

blessings, 15

Canada, 16

candles, 12, 15

ceremonies, 16

concerts, 16

dates, 11

dreidel, 27, 28

Eiffel Tower, 19

Feast of Dedication, 11

Festival of Lights, 11

foods, 24, 28

France, 16, 19

gifts, 27

Hebrew language, 27

Israel, 16, 19

Jerusalem, 19

Jewish people, 3, 4, 7, 16, 20, 23, 27

latkes, 24, 28

Maccabees, 7–8

menorahs, 12, 15, 16, 19, 20

oil lamps, 8

parades, 16

parties, 28

rededication, 8

Russia, 16, 20

shamash, 12, 15

songs, 23, 28

sufganiyot, 24

temples, 4, 8

torch race, 19

United States, 16

About the Author

Trudi Strain Trueit is a former television news reporter and weather forecaster. She has written more than thirty fiction and nonfiction books for children. Ms. Trueit lives near Seattle, Washington, with her husband Bill.

Photo Credits

Photographs © 2007: Bridgeman Art Library International Ltd., London/New York/Ashmolean Museum, University of Oxford, UK: 9, 31 top right; Corbis Images: 3, 30 top left (Charles Gupton), 18 (Richard T. Nowitz), 29, 30 top right (Royalty-Free); Index Stock Imagery/David Wasserman: 14, 31 bottom left; Israelimages.com: 25 (Yuval Gilad), 22 (Cathy Raff); Landov, LLC/John Gillis/UPI: 17; Superstock, Inc.: cover (Brand X), 13, 31 top left (Shaffer/Smith); The Art Archive/Picture Desk/Dagli Orti/Bibliothèque Municipale Valenciennes: 6, 30 bottom right; The Image Works: 26, 30 bottom left (Li-Hua Lan/Syracuse Newspapers), 21 (Tony Savino), 5, 31 bottom right (David Wells).